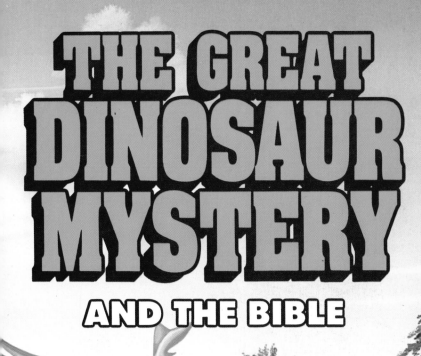

THE GREAT DINOSAUR MYSTERY

AND THE BIBLE

PAUL S. TAYLOR

MB
MASTER BOOK PUBLISHERS
San Diego, California

The Great Dinosaur Mystery and the Bible

Copyright ©1987, Paul S. Taylor and Films for Christ Association

First Printing, February 1987

Second Printing, May 1987

Third Printing, August 1987

Fourth Printing, November 1987

Fifth Printing, December 1987

Sixth Printing, May 1988

Seventh Printing, December 1988

MASTER BOOKS

A Division of CLP, Inc.

P.O. Box 1606

El Cajon, California, 92022

Library of Congress Catalog Card Number
ISBN 0-89051-114-4

Cataloging in Publication Data

Taylor, Paul Stanley, 1953-

Great Dinosaur Mystery and The Bible

1. Dinosauria—Juvenile literature.
2. Paleontology.

CONTENTS

DINOSAURS

Long ago dinosaurs both big and small roamed planet Earth. Today there are many mysteries to be solved about these marvelous animals. What did they really look like? Why did they die out? Has anyone ever seen a live dinosaur? How do dinosaurs fit into the Bible? What do their fossils tell about our planet?

Scientists have uncovered lots of exciting new information about dinosaurs. Answers are being found to questions that have puzzled people for years. More dinosaur fossils are being found in more places around the world than ever before.

So much is new that a lot of what has been written about dinosaurs in the past is being changed. Many old ideas and drawings are outdated.

Footprints

FOSSIL CLUES

WHY IS SO LITTLE KNOWN ABOUT DINOSAURS?

Despite all the new dinosaur discoveries, many mysteries have not been solved. Why? Because almost all information has to come from ancient bones and footprints—fossils.

Just what are fossils? A fossil is an ancient dead animal or plant—or something left by them. Usually they are found buried in mud or sand that turned into rock. Now, thousands of years later, we find them in the rock layers of the earth. If the fossil is petrified, rock has replaced parts of the plant or animal.

Claws

Dung (coprolite)

Eggs, sometimes with unborn babies

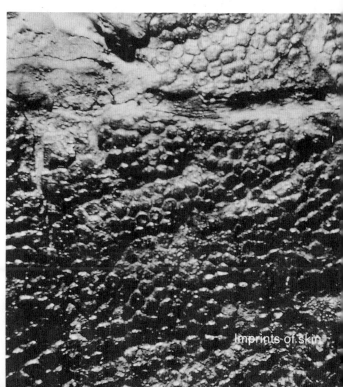

Imprints of skin

10

WHAT KINDS OF DINOSAUR FOSSILS HAVE BEEN FOUND?

Bones
Teeth
Claws
Spikes
Horns
Bony plates
Eggs, sometimes with unborn babies
"Gizzard" stones (gastroliths)
Dung (coprolite)
Footprints
Imprints of skin (very rare)
Stomach contents (very rare)

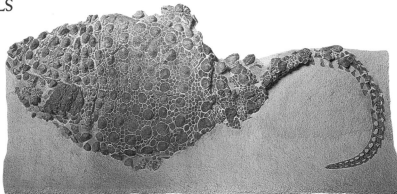

Bony plates

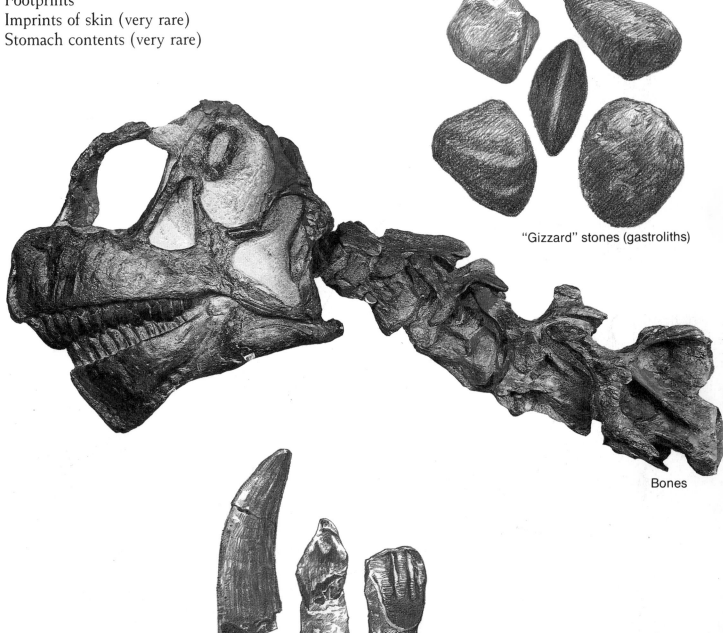

"Gizzard" stones (gastroliths)

Bones

Teeth

THE WRONG-HEADED
DINOSAUR

Even the great *Brontosaurus* (BRAHN-toe-SOR-us) has changed. This is the dinosaur most people know best. Millions have seen it in books and advertising. Unfortunately, the *Brontosaurus* never really existed—even though it was pictured in every dinosaur book and museum for the last hundred years.

The dinosaur was discovered with the head missing. To make the skeleton complete, a scientist added a skull found three or four miles away. But no one else knew this. The skeleton actually belonged to a type of *Diplodocus* (Dip-LAHD-oh-kuss). The skull was from an *Apatosaurus* (Ah-PAT-oh-SOR-us).

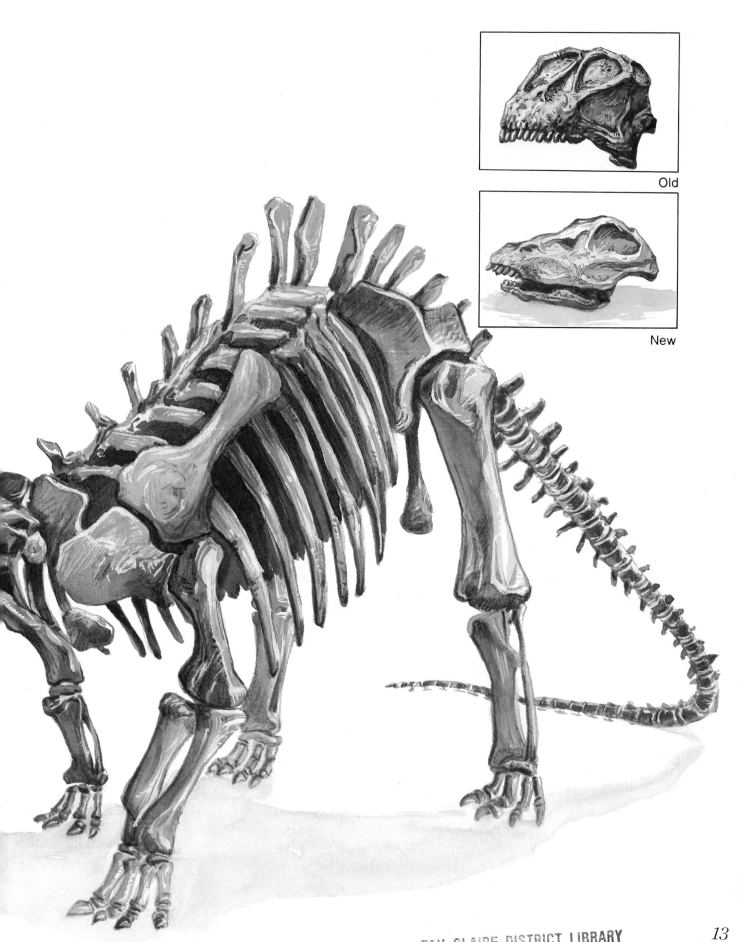

Old

New

13

THE PROBLEM WITH FOSSILS

Putting a dinosaur skeleton together is not easy. It is often like putting together a very difficult jigsaw puzzle with many of the pieces missing or damaged. The skeletons are usually very incomplete. Many dinosaur fossils are discovered badly damaged. Bones are often found crushed or bent by the great weight of the dirt and rock above. Sometimes parts from different creatures are mixed together. This just adds to the confusion.

Unfortunately, some scientists have not been careful enough in their descriptions of dinosaurs. They have told grand stories of how dinosaurs looked and behaved. All of these descriptions are based on guesswork—the imaginations of people who have never seen a living dinosaur.

Some scientists have made complete pictures of dinosaurs based on just a single bone or tooth or leg. Such pictures are based on many guesses and very little facts. The scientists' ideas often turn out to be wrong when more facts are discovered.

Dinosaur fossils are not found with labels or photographs attached showing what the animals looked like. That is why no pictures of dinosaurs in this book or any other are exactly right. Every dinosaur painting is sure to contain at least some wrong information. No artist ever saw the living, breathing animals—complete with skin, flesh and color.

For instance, imagine never having seen or heard of a poodle or a peacock. One day you find the jumbled bones of one buried in the ground. You try to put the bones together to form a skeleton. And then you try to draw a picture of what the animal looked like when alive. But bones cannot tell the whole story. Even if you are a very good artist, it would be a miracle if you drew a true picture of a poodle or a peacock just from the bones and your imagination.

If scientists could climb into a time machine and travel to the past, they could get much better information. Only then would they know the true appearance of dinosaurs or what they ate and how they really behaved. Scientists might be very surprised at what they would learn.

Dinosaur Bones

Poodle Bones

Peacock Bones

14

WHERE DID DINOSAURS COME FROM?

When God created the world, dinosaurs were one of His creations. God created all the animals (Genesis 1:20-25). God made everything in the entire universe—people, stars, planets and all that there is (Exodus 20:11a, Genesis 1, John 1:3). Like Adam, the bodies of the first dinosaurs were formed from the dust of the earth. Man and dinosaurs lived at the same time.

17

ARE DINOSAURS
IN THE BIBLE?

Dinosaur-like creatures are mentioned in the Bible. The Bible uses ancient names like "behemoth" (beh-HEE-moth) and "tannin." Behemoth means kingly, gigantic beasts. Tannin is a term which includes dragon-like animals and the great sea creatures such as whales, giant squids, and marine reptiles like the plesiosaurs (PLEE-see-oh-sors) that may have become extinct (died out).

The Bible's best description of a dinosaur-like animal is in Job chapter 40.

Look at the behemoth, which I made along with you and which feeds on grass like an ox. What strength he has in his loins, what power in the muscles of his belly! His tail sways like a cedar; the sinews of his thighs are close-knit. His bones are tubes of bronze, his limbs like rods of iron. He ranks first among the works of God . . .

Job 40:15-19 (NIV)

18

The book of Job is very old, probably written around 2,000 years before Jesus was born. Here God describes a great king of the land animals like some of the biggest dinosaurs, the *Diplodocus* and *Apatosaurus*. It was a gigantic plant-eater with great muscles and very strong bones. The long *Diplodocus* had leg bones so strong that he could have held three others on his back.

The behemoth were not afraid. They did not need to be; they were huge. Behemah tails were so long and strong that God compared them to cedars—one of the largest and most spectacular trees of the ancient world.

After all the behemoth had died out, many people forgot about them. Dinosaurs were extinct and the fossil skeletons that are in museums today did not begin to be put together until about 150 years ago. Today, some people have mistakenly guessed that the behemah mentioned in the Bible might be an elephant or a hippopotamus. But those animals certainly do not have tails like the thick, tall trunks of cedar trees!

19

WHY DID GOD CREATE DINOSAURS?

All animals, including the first dinosaurs, were created to benefit mankind in one way or another. God's exact purpose for the various dinosaurs is still a mystery. Perhaps the larger dinosaurs kept certain types of lush plant life under control and cleared paths through the forest. Using their long necks, some dinosaurs could have eaten foliage at the tops of tall trees. In a thick forest, this would let light come down to the ground so smaller plants would have a chance to grow.

God brought many animals to Adam for his personal inspection; the dinosaurs may have been included. God watched to see what Adam thought of all these wonderful creatures. He waited while Adam made up a name for each one (Genesis 2:19). Each new animal must have been a fun surprise. Why did God invent so many different kinds of beautiful, interesting and surprising animals? Perhaps because He wanted to delight Man with His power, wisdom and love.

Part of God's purpose for creating the particular types of dinosaurs that became very large was surely to impress Man. Dinosaurs showed the great power of the Creator. No matter how big these creatures got, Adam knew God was always far greater. God designed every part of them, right down to the smallest cell. Even the largest dinosaur was like an obedient puppy in God's wise, powerful hands.

WHAT WAS LIFE WITH DINOSAURS LIKE, AT FIRST?

The first man and woman, Adam and Eve, were close friends of God. And they were masters over all His wonderful creatures (Genesis 1:26,28). Adam and his family were meant to enjoy the animals and rule over them forever with love.

In those first, early days the earth was a beautiful paradise. Everything was happy and perfect—just as God intended. Wouldn't it be wonderful to have lived in those days? There were delicious fruits and plants of all types to eat. They were probably much better than the kinds available today.

All of the animals were friendly and under Man's control. None of the animals ate meat or killed. God provided the plants and seeds with all the vitamins people and animals needed. There was no sin, no death or evil or disease.

21

WHY DID DINOSAURS BECOME EXTINCT?

There have been many ideas to explain why dinosaurs became extinct. At least 55 different theories have been suggested and then thrown out because of problems. For instance, a theory that works for large animals usually does not explain the extinction of small animals or sea creatures. Whatever happened to dinosaurs, scientists agree that it must have affected the whole world.

WERE THE DINOSAURS KILLED BY A METEORITE?

The latest dinosaur extinction theory suggests that the earth was struck from space by a six-mile-wide meteorite (a comet or asteroid). Such a collision could have left a huge layer of dust in the atmosphere. The dust could have been enough to block out the sun's light for months and perhaps years. Because most plants need lots of sunlight, this would have destroyed many of them. The dinosaurs would have starved on a cold, darkened planet.

What is wrong with this theory? Scientists have found no crater hole where the

supposed meteorite struck the earth. And, if the meteorite collision really happened, why did other forms of life survive—including birds, small vertebrates (including mammals), big crocodiles, insects, flowering plants, freshwater plants and animals, various types of sea life, etc.?

The only evidence for this great collision from space comes from certain layers of clay with a metal called iridium in them. Asteroids have this element. However, this does not necessarily mean that the deposits had to come from the explosion of a single asteroid.

Also, the earth's core has this metal in it. Iridium can be brought up by volcanos that erupt. Could some of these deposits of metal be evidence of large volcanic eruptions of iridium in the past? It is interesting that some Christian scientists believe that most of the dinosaurs were killed and buried during a relatively short period of time. And during this time, they believe, the earth was probably in the midst of the greatest earthquakes and volcanic eruptions ever known.

No matter where each of the iridium deposits came from, it is important to notice they all had something in common. The iridium was buried in the midst of tons of hardened mud and sands called sediment. Such thick layers of sediment suggest that something more than asteroids was involved in the death and extinction of dinosaurs.

WHERE DID MOST OF THE DINOSAUR FOSSILS COME FROM?

The Bible tells of a great flood that covered the entire earth—Noah's Flood. This was the greatest disaster in history. Nothing else has even come close. The Flood waters rose above all the world's mountains and killed most of the air-breathing, land animals and all but eight people in Noah's family (Genesis 6:12-13, 7:21-23). It destroyed the entire surface of the earth (Genesis 9:11).

Great supplies of water stored underground came bursting out (Genesis 7:11, 8:2). The earth's crust heaved and buckled unleashing terrible volcanic eruptions and massive earthquakes like the world has never seen before or since.

Rain poured out from dark, thundering skies in unending torrents. Waves of loosened earth and trees slid down hillsides burying plants by the thousands. All of the cities were totally destroyed. And so was God's garden in Eden. For forty days the rains continued. And the waves continued to rise, fed by vast amounts of underground water which used to feed the rivers and springs of the world, including the Garden in the land of Eden (Genesis 2:6, 10-14).

Under the pressure of this worldwide disaster, the earth shook again and again causing huge tidal waves to sweep across the sinking land. So great was the destruction that every human being died and with them, millions of animals and plants.

The only people spared were Noah's family. According to God's instructions, Noah built a great barge-shaped boat to save his family and thousands of animals to be used to refill the earth. God protected this precious ship and its passengers throughout the disaster which lasted over a year.

When the destruction was finished, peace slowly began to return to the earth. Eventually, the waters dropped to a level safe enough for Noah and his family to leave the Ark on dry ground (Genesis 8:13, 14).

Such a great event would surely have left evidence to be found today. For instance, one would expect to find billions of dead creatures buried by water in mud and sand (now hardened to rock). And that is exactly what scientists do find around the world.

Thousands of dinosaur bones can be found where they were washed together by violent flood waters and buried under mud, sand and rock. Many of the animals were torn apart and their bones broken and jumbled-up. The muds and sands hardened like concrete to form the great layers of fossil rocks we find today.

Quick flood burial would be the only way that so many dinosaurs and other things could have become fossilized in the way scientists have found them. Animals and plants will fossilize only if they are buried quickly and deeply—before predators, decay and weather destroy them.

DOESN'T IT TAKE MILLIONS OF YEARS FOR A DINOSAUR BONE TO BECOME A FOSSIL?

Just because something is "fossilized" does not mean that it is millions (or even thousands) of years old. When the conditions and materials are right, a bone can become filled with minerals fairly quickly. The main ingredients are:

1. Quick burial.
2. Water, in the right amounts.
3. Suitable minerals.

Conditions during the Flood were ideal for "fossilizing" millions of animals and plants.

Researchers have found that chicken bones and wood can be replaced with minerals in just five to ten years. A big dinosaur bone might take hundreds of years to completely mineralize. It all depends on the burial conditions over the years.

Many dinosaur remains are still not completely turned to rock. More than half of the fossil is still original bone, not stone! Some even have chemicals from the living animals (proteins and amino acids)! Some fish fossils still have a fishy smell when first uncovered.

Some of the plants buried during the Flood are not fossilized either. In New Jersey, large amounts of wood from trees that were growing at the same time as dinosaurs can be found buried in dirt (Cretaceous clay). They are preserved, but not turned to stone at all. In England, fragile plant hairs and tiny details of the plant's cells can be seen. The plants are not turned into rock. They are just flattened and blackened. Since the Flood happened only about four to five thousand years ago, these types of discoveries are not surprising.

Author points to dinosaur bones found in Wyoming (USA). When some dinosaur fossils are cut with a diamond saw, the distinct odor of burning bone can be smelled. Most of the fossil is still bone and still contains chemicals from when the animals were alive.

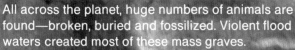

All across the planet, huge numbers of animals are found—broken, buried and fossilized. Violent flood waters created most of these mass graves.

WHY DID GOD SEND THE FLOOD?

The Bible says that before the Flood people became very, very sinful. There was so much evil that God was sorry that He made Man (Genesis 6:6-7). The earth had become a terrible place. People thought only about evil things all the time. Life was full of fear, terror and evil.

The Creator's heart was filled with pain at all the horrible wickedness. In His mercy, He ended Man's suffering in this sin-polluted world with the swift judgment of the Flood.

God destroyed all the evil people and their whole sinful world. He used the Flood to bury their evil cities and all their wicked belongings. He wiped out practically every trace of them. The destruction was so great that it changed the world's environment and geography until this day. This is a reminder to everyone that God really does punish sin.

But God did remember the good people. There were only eight of them, but He saved them. God blessed Noah's family and used them to give the human race a wonderful, fresh start. Every person living today came from one of Noah's three sons—Shem, Ham and Japheth.

DID NOAH TAKE DINOSAURS ON BOARD THE ARK?

The Bible does not list the names of every creature on the Ark. It does say that one set of every kind of air-breathing land animal was on board (Genesis 6:19-20, 7:15-16). So, dinosaurs must have been included.

There is evidence that dinosaurs lived after the Flood. For instance, Job saw "behemoth" after the Flood. (Other evidences will be discussed later.)

The Ark was a very large ship designed especially by God for its important purpose. It was so large and complex that it took Noah 120 years to build. Noah used this time to warn people about the Flood and convince them to turn to God and be saved with his family.

The Ark had plenty of room for all the animals, including the dinosaurs. It was carefully built to fulfill the needs of each passenger as they rested in safety during the great Flood. Many of the animals may have slept through most of the trip.

Noah did not have to go out and find the animals. God brought each one. This probably included a young pair of each main type of dinosaur. Perhaps God just included the basic kinds of dinosaurs He first created; not every variety that had developed since Creation.

Young dinosaurs would be small and easier to care for and would use less food. It would have been foolish to fill up space on the Ark with the oldest, biggest adults.

33

AFTER THE FLOOD, WHAT HAPPENED TO DINOSAURS?

When the Flood was over Noah opened the Ark's big door and let the animals free. Babies were born to each set of parents. After many years, the earth began to be filled with animals again.

The dinosaurs lived for at least a few centuries after the Flood, but probably never in the great numbers that there had once been. No one knows exactly when they finally died out.

After the Flood the earth was a very different place. When Noah stepped off the ship, it must have felt like getting out on another planet. Nothing would have looked familiar. Most of the world was left covered with water. Seven out of every ten spots on the globe are still under water today.

All the landmarks were destroyed. The Garden in Eden was gone forever. So was the whole land of Eden and every other land. Mud and rock were everywhere. Cold, forbidding mountains stood where none had been before.

Earthquakes and volcanos continued to plague animals and man, even after the Flood was over—and still do today on a smaller scale.

Temperatures had become extreme. Some parts of the world got much hotter after the Flood. This eventually dried up all the water and left great deserts. In other places, snow began to fall for the first time because of freezing cold. A short ice "age" followed the Flood in some parts of the world.

Harmful radiation from the sun (and space) probably came down in much larger doses after the Flood. The original world may have been protected from this radiation by a special atmosphere. The earth's air may have contained a much higher amount of water which kept the weather warmer and more pleasant. Before the Flood, plants were watered by rivers, underground springs and dew—instead of by rain.

After the Flood, many parts of the world became too harsh for dinosaurs. No longer did the earth have the same great forests of huge, nutritious plants. It would have been hard for the dinosaurs to locate enough food as they got bigger and bigger.

It was not just the dinosaurs that died off. Great numbers of creatures have become extinct in the thousands of years since the Flood. In the last 350 years alone, almost 400 species have disappeared. Today, some experts claim that one or more species of plants and animals may be lost every day. Most of the problem is caused by sinful and foolish human beings.

Today, many animals are only being saved by zoos. Dinosaurs became extinct long before people worried about such things.

The Flood and the changes it caused in the environment are the main reason dinosaurs died off. However, sinful people may have caused dinosaur deaths in an even more direct way.

Man has often been responsible for killing the last animals of a kind. The mammoths and mastodons were wiped out by hunters. It could be that in ancient times, people also killed dinosaurs for meat or because of problems these animals caused. Maybe some killing was done just for sport.

DRAGONS AND DINOSAURS

Ancient peoples all over the world have told of unusual, reptile-like creatures that once roamed the earth. There were many different types, both large and small. And there were many different names for them. The ancient people of Europe called them "dragons." Many ancient descriptions of dragons sound like dinosaurs.

The ancient, original "dragon" legends must have come from memories of dinosaurs.

Scientists agree that legends are almost always based on facts, not just pure imagination. It cannot be an accident that so many separate peoples of the world tell such stories.

"Dragon" legends and pictures can be found in Africa, India, Europe, the Middle East, the Orient and every other part of the world. Dinosaur-like animals have been drawn, written about and told about since the beginning of recorded history.

Many pictures of dragons look very much like known dinosaurs or similar animals. Other, more strange dragon pictures look like composite drawings of various types of dinosaurs. The horns, spikes, tails, armor, heads, and legs of different dinosaurs can be put together in many ways to make fairy-tale dragons just like those in some of the old paintings and stories.

Left to right, starting at the top left:
1. St. George and a dragon. 15th century A.D.
2. Dragon head. 16th century A.D.
3. St. George and a dragon. 15th century A.D.
4. *Ornitholestes* (or-nith-oh-LESS-teez)
5. *Saurolophus* (Sor-oh-LOAF-us)
6. *Rutiodon* (RU-tee-o-don)

Sometimes people in olden times made up scary or funny stories about these animals. This made the "dragons" and their hunters seem even more special. Some of the stories really got wild and crazy.

Most of the dragon legends are full of exaggeration, magic and marvelous deeds. But this is not true of all of them. Many stories seem rather believable.

Did some of these storytellers see live dinosaurs? Which stories are based on real encounters? And which are merely fairy tales based on the stories of others? Will anyone ever know for sure?

Babylon

One "dragon" story from the ancient land of Sumer in Babylon tells of the hero Gilgamesh. He decided to make a name for himself by traveling to a distant land to cut great cedar trees needed for his city. He reached the forest with fifty volunteers and discovered a huge reptile-like animal which ate trees and reeds. The story simply says that Gilgamesh killed it and cut off its head for a trophy.

Ancient Roman mosaic showing two long-necked dragons by the sea. 2nd century A.D.

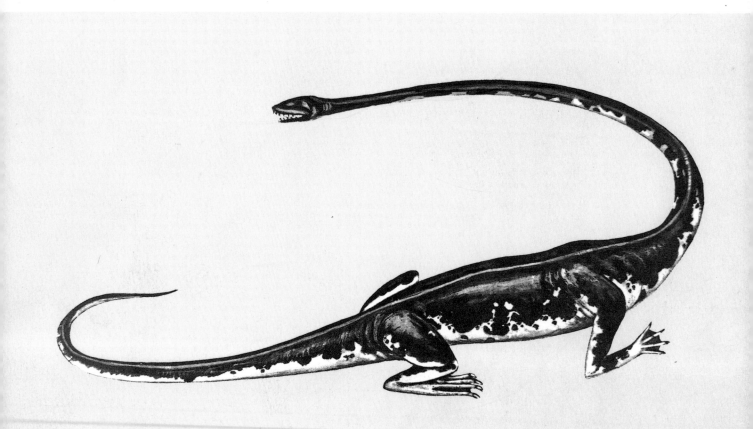

Tanystropheus (TAN-ee-STROH-fee-us)

An ancient Indian carving. Is it a dinosaur? No one knows for sure. The etching in rock was discovered on a wall of the Grand Canyon. *(White outline added for clarity.)* Compare this, for example, to the dinosaur Edmontosaurus. On the same canyon wall, carvings have been reported of what seem to be people, an elephant, a wooly rhinoceros and an ibex.

Scandinavia

One old legend describes a reptile-like animal that had a body about the size of a large cow. Its two back legs were long and strong. But its front legs were remarkably short. And its jaws were quite large. One of the unique things about many dinosaurs was their short front legs, compared to their long, strong back legs. Many also had large jaws. Examples of dinosaurs which fit are the *Edmontosaurus* (ed-MONT-oh-SOR-us), *Iguanodon* (i-GWA-no-DON), *Tyrannosaurus* (tie-RAN-oh-SOR-us), etc.

EDMONTOSAURUS

Edmontosaurus (Ed-MONT-oh-SOR-us)   39

France

The city of Nerluc was renamed in honor of the killing of a "dragon" there. This animal was bigger than an ox and had long, sharp, pointed horns on its head. There were a number of different horned dinosaurs. The *Triceratops* (try-SER-ah-tops) is one example.

Europe

A well-known, old science book, the *Historia Animalium*, claims that "dragons" were still not extinct in the 1500's. But the animals were said to be extremely rare and relatively small by then.

Italy

A scientist named Ulysses Aldrovandus carefully described a small "dragon" seen along a farm road in northern Italy. The date was May 13, 1572. The poor, rare creature was so little that a farmer killed it just by knocking it on the head with his walking stick. The animal had done nothing wrong but hiss at the farmer's oxen as they approached it on the road.

The scientist got the dead body and made measurements and a drawing. He even had the animal mounted for a museum. It had a long neck, a very long tail and a fat body. The skeletons of a number of ancient reptile-like creatures match this basic description.

41

China

Thousands of dragon stories and pictures can be found in ancient Chinese books and art. One interesting legend tells about a famous Chinese man named Yu. After the great world flood, Yu surveyed the land of China and divided it into sections. He "built channels to drain the water off to the sea" and helped make the land livable again. Many snakes and "dragons" were driven from the marshlands when Yu created the new farmlands.

Some old Chinese books even tell of a family that kept "dragons" and raised the babies. It is said that in those days, Chinese kings used "dragons" for pulling royal chariots on special occasions.

Ireland (c. 900 A.D.)

An Irish writer recorded an encounter with a large beast with "iron" nails on its tail which pointed backwards. Its head was shaped a little bit like a horse's. And it had thick legs with strong claws. These details match features of dinosaurs like the *Kentrosaurus* (KEN-tro-SOR-us) and *Stegosaurus* (STEG-oh-SOR-us). They had sharp-pointed spines on their tails, thick legs, strong claws and long skulls.

43

Africa and Arabia (c. 460 B.C.)

The respected Greek explorer Herodotus described small flying reptiles in ancient Egypt and Arabia. These animals sound amazingly like the small *Rhamphorhynchus* (RAM-foe-RING-kus). They had the same snake-like body and bat-like wings. Many had been killed near the city of Buto (Arabia). He was shown a canyon with many piles of their back-bones and ribs.

Herodotus said that these animals could sometimes be found in the spice groves. They were "small in size and of various colors." Large numbers would sometimes gather in the frankincense trees. When workers wanted to gather the trees' valuable juices, they would use smelly smoke to drive the flying reptiles away.

The well-respected Greek, Aristotle, said that in his time it was common knowledge that creatures like this also existed in Ethiopia. Similar animals (three feet long) were also described in India by the geographer Strabo.

ARE ANY DINOSAURS ALIVE TODAY?

There is some evidence that a few dinosaurs and great marine reptiles could still be alive, teetering on the edge of extinction. Scientists are still discovering unknown animals every year.

Natives in a very remote jungle in Africa have repeatedly told of seeing large animals a lot like the sauropod dinosaurs. The sauropods included the *Apatosaurus, Brachiosaurus, Diplodocus,* and others like them.

A group of natives may have killed a small one in 1959. Some scientists have studied the reports and are planning trips into the deep jungle. They hope to find a dinosaur still alive.

"Dragons" of the Air

Great numbers of pterosaurs (TARE-oh-SORS) were killed by the Flood. These were sometimes large, but delicate, flying reptiles. Many of their fossils have been found. Are all the pterosaurs in the world dead today? Probably, but scientists still don't know for sure. In Africa, a scientist found evidence that a few might still be alive.

Natives living in northern Zimbabwe described a strange flying animal which they called the "kongamato." It was not a bird but more like a reddish-colored lizard with bare, bat-like wings. The distance between its wingtips was four to seven feet.

The scientist showed the natives pictures of various animals, both living and extinct. Each person interviewed said the *Pterodactyl* (TEH-ro-DAK-till) was most like the kongamoto. These animals are supposed to live mainly in a huge, dense area called the Jiunda Swamp. Researchers have heard of animals like this in other places, too.

45

"Dragons" of the Sea

Like fish, the great reptiles of the sea could have lived through the Flood without being taken on the Ark. Noah was told to protect land-dwelling animals and birds, not fish and other creatures that could survive in the floodwaters.

An ancient Hebrew legend says that the only animals to survive the Flood, besides those on the Ark, were "the giant og, the monster reem and the fishes." The word "og" means gigantic and long-necked—a good description of the big plesiosaurs.

In 1977, the nets of a Japanese fishing ship, the Zuiyo Maru, caught the decaying body of a large, strange reptile near New Zealand. Photographs, measurements and tissue samples all show that it was probably one of the great marine reptiles like the *Plesiosaurus* (PLEE-see-o-SOR-us).

Unfortunately, they threw the carcass back into the sea because of the smell and decay. But it is not likely this ship happened to catch the very last one. Others are probably still alive.

In every part of the world, ships have made reports of animals like this and other types of unknown creatures. Most scientists agree there are probably many more sea creatures to be discovered. Man knows more about the surface of the moon than he does about life in the world's great oceans. There is more sworn evidence for "sea monsters" than would be needed to prove any ordinary case in a court of law.

The Navy ship U.S.S. Stein tangled with such a creature on its way to track submarines near South America. When its sonar equipment suddenly stopped working, the captain headed the ship back for repairs at the Long Beach Naval Dockyard. When the tough underwater sonar dome was examined in dry dock the crew found a big surprise. The rubber covering that protects the dome was torn and battered with dozens of big gouges.

Hundreds of sharp, hollow teeth (or claws) were left broken off in the covering. Some were longer than an inch.

It looked as if some large sea creature had been attracted to the underwater sounds of the sonar and tried to bite it and break it. After months of examination, scientists at the Naval Oceans Center made a decision. The animal "must have been extremely large and of a species still unknown to science."

(Right) Decayed body of a possible modern plesiosaur snagged 900-feet underwater near Christchurch, New Zealand (April 10, 1977). 32-feet long / weight, approximately 4000-pounds / 4 fins, each approximately 3-feet long. The evidence was examined and tested by a committee of high-ranking Japanese marine scientists. The Director of Animal Research at the National Science Museum of Japan said, "It seems that these animals are not extinct after all. It's impossible for only one to have survived. There must be a group."

(Below) So important was this find that the Japanese honored it with a commerative postage stamp. As the scientific discovery of the year, the plesiosaur was used as the official emblem for the 1977 National Exhibition which celebrated 100-years of scientific discovery.

Leviathan

The "leviathan" the Bible talks about in Job 41 is described as the greatest creature in the sea. Unlike a crocodile or fish, it was useless to try to catch a leviathan with hooks, harpoons or anything else. "Nothing on Earth is his equal—a creature without fear" (Job 41:33, NIV).

What was leviathan? The large size, strong jaws, great teeth, fast swimming ability and its protected back and undersides all give clues. It could have been a *Kronosaurus* (KRONE-oh-SOR-us) or something like it. This was one of the greatest, most overwhelming animals ever to swim the seas. It was not a true dinosaur, but it was reptile-like and had great, sharp teeth.

It seems these animals were still alive at the time of King David. Psalm 104 says they played where the ships go to and fro. This was probably in the Mediterranean Sea.

It is interesting that many reports of "sea serpents" closely match the ancient pliosaurs and mosasaurs. They looked somewhat like huge lizards or crocodiles with flippers or webbed feet. Fossils show their backbones were very flexible. They could probably swim with a snake-like motion.

Kronosaurus (left), *plesiosaur* (right).

A creature very much like these was reported during World War I by a German submarine. Captain Georg von Forstner described what happened:

"On July 30, 1915, our *U28* torpedoed the British steamer *Iberian* carrying a rich cargo in the North Atlantic. The steamer sank quickly, the bow sticking almost vertically into the air. When it had gone for about twenty-five seconds there was a violent explosion. A little later pieces of wreckage, and among them a gigantic sea animal (writhing and struggling wildly), was shot out of the water to a height of 60 to 100-feet. At that moment I had with me in the conning tower my officers of the watch, the chief engineer, the navigator, and the helmsman. Simultaneously we all drew one another's attention to this wonder of the seas . . . we were unable to identify it. We did not have the time to take a photograph, for the animal sank out of sight after ten or fifteen seconds. It was about 60-feet long, was like a crocodile in shape and had four limbs with powerful webbed feet and a long tail tapering to a point."

49

DINOSAURS AND
THE LOST PARADISE

It is interesting to think about the original world God created. Things have changed so much since then. Everything was perfect, but then came sin. God warned Adam and Eve not to eat from the Tree of the Knowledge of Good and Evil. They were told that if they disobeyed, something very bad would happen—and it did. Adam's disobedience was deliberate and wrong. To this day, all people continue to disobey God in many different ways.

Sin ruined the perfect beauty of God's Creation and brought trouble, death, suffering and other bad things into all of Man's kingdom (Genesis 3:16-24, Romans 5:12, 8:20-22, I Corinthians 15:21-22). Thorns and thistles, disease-producing germs and blood-sucking parasites, fighting and killing—all developed sometime after the first sin.

DID ANIMALS EAT MEAT *BEFORE* THE FLOOD?

Today, there are many animals that kill other animals for food. Exactly when this habit first began is a mystery. But it could not have started until sometime after Man's first sin. In the original Creation, all the animals ate plants, not meat (Genesis 1:30). There was no killing before the Fall (when Adam and Eve rebelled against God in the Garden of Eden). It was not until sometime after sin's "beginning" that animals began to eat other animals.

Did this habit begin right after Man's first sin? Probably not. It is certainly not likely that animals *instantly* changed into the way they are today. These habits probably developed naturally in Man's sinful world over hundreds and thousands of years. And they may not have become common until sometime after the Flood.

Before the Flood, there is no indication in the Bible that any of the animals ate meat or were violent and vicious. It is the people that God says were so terrible and violent.

By the time of the Flood, most animals must still have been able to live on plant foods alone. Every basic kind of land animal and bird in the world was on the Ark. They ate only plants during the voyage. For God told Noah to load the ship with every kind of food the animals would need (Genesis 6:21). These foods must have been the same things God assigned to the animals in the beginning—"every green plant."

There is no hint that God changed this command between the time of Creation and the Flood. Before the Flood, there may have been no need for animals to kill each other for food.

Parasaurolophus (PAR-ah-SOR-oh-LOAF-us), a hadrosaur. Many different types of these duck-billed dinosaurs have been found. The fossilized stomach of one shows the last meal it ate during (or just before) the Flood. Before being killed and buried, it ate fruits, seeds, pine needles and pine cones.

WHEN DID ANIMALS BEGIN TO KILL AND EAT OTHER ANIMALS?

After the Flood, God gave people official permission to kill animals for food and eat them. Man could now eat everything, green plants *and* animals (Genesis 9:2,3). This means that people from Noah's family could have eaten dinosaurs, if they tasted good.

But God told the animals (including dinosaurs) that they should not kill people. If they did, they would have to answer to God for it (Genesis 9:5b).

At the same time, the Bible does not say that animals were forbidden to kill other animals for food in this new world. God does not repeat His command, here or later, that animals are to eat plants. So, it could be that the end of the Flood marks the time when land animals and birds began to develop the habit of killing for food. Or, it might just be the time when these habits started to become more common.

In the world before the Flood some animals must have died from natural causes. For example, some must have been killed by injuries, like falls from trees. Other animals would surely find these dead bodies and smell them. Could it be that some animals, also, decided to taste the bodies and even eat them?

Actually, this would have been a good thing. It would be best to have a quick way to get rid of dead, smelly bodies in the world after the Fall. Today, it is important for animals to do this.

So, it could be that animals ate dead animals once in a while before the Flood, but that few (if any) animals killed for food until sometime after the Flood. This seems to make sense, since the fossils show the pre-Flood world had plenty of plants to eat. The animals probably did not need to kill to live.

Meat-eating would have been encouraged by the Flood. The Flood was the world's greatest disaster. It destroyed all of the world's huge, lush forests of plant life. Until new forests grew, there was much less food. The Flood would have left a certain number of decaying animal bodies unburied on the earth's surface. The bodies would have been tempting meals for hungry, sharp-toothed animals.

It must have been much harder to survive in the world after the Flood. Since food was no longer so abundant, some animals were forced to compete. This would cause quarrels and fights, even among animals in the same family.

Plants growing in the soils of the destroyed earth would have had less protein and vitamins than before, especially in certain areas of the world. With an increasing taste for meat, hunger could have driven some animals to kill for food, instead of waiting for dead bodies to turn up. Animals needed to feed their hungry families. Hunger and starvation can make some creatures desperate and vicious.

What an awful thing sin did to God's wonderful, peaceful Creation!

THE TERRIBLE EFFECTS OF SINFUL DISOBEDIENCE

Ever since Adam and Eve, Man's whole environment has forced him to see just how serious sin is. Adam's disobedience ultimately changed all of his kingdom for the worse (Romans 8:20-22, Genesis 3:14-19). The effects of sin are everywhere. As the apostle Paul said, "The whole creation has been groaning in pain right up to the present time" (Romans 8:22).

WERE THE DINOSAURS EVER REALLY AS FEROCIOUS AS THEY ARE SHOWN IN BOOKS AND FILMS?

There is another mystery about dinosaurs to be explored. Today, many books and movies show dinosaurs as terrible, ferocious beasts. But since there are only fossils to study today, there is no way to know for sure how dinosaurs behaved.

Most dinosaurs had small brains in comparison to the size of their bodies. The 29-foot long *Stegosaurus* had a brain the size of a walnut. Even the great *Apatosaurus's* brain was not much larger than a kitten's. If a huge *Brachiosaurus* (BRACK-ee-o-SOR-us) could be shrunk to the size of a human, its brain would be 10,000 times smaller than Man's. This does not necessarily mean these dinosaurs were stupid as animals go, but they were surely no match for Man's brain.

Many of the dinosaurs were quite small. The *Saltopus* (SALT-oh-puss) was really tiny—no bigger than a housecat. Most of the dinosaurs killed by the Flood were less than fifteen feet long, not including their tails which made them more than twice as long. In museums, most people never see the small dinosaurs because the jumbo-sized ones are so much more impressive.

And, of course, all *young* dinosaurs were small. If they were born from eggs, they were very little. No one knows for sure if all dinosaurs laid eggs, but they may have. The eggs that have been found are never very big. The larger they are, the stronger and thicker the shell has to be. This made it harder for the baby dinosaur to get out. Eggs from medium-size dinosaurs are never much bigger than a turkey's egg. No one has found an egg from a great *Brachiosaurus* or *Apatosaurus*, but eggs were discovered from the 39-foot-long *Hypselosaurus* (HIP-se-loh-SOR-us). This dinosaur's shape was somewhat like the *Apatosaurus*. Its biggest egg was only 12 inches long.

It probably took the big dinosaurs a very long lifetime to reach great size. Perhaps like the people before the Flood, dinosaurs also had long lives. One man, Methuselah, lived 969 years in those days of better health and environment. Adam and Eve were originally created with perfect hearts and eyes, perfect hearing and health—perfect bodies in every way. And so were the animals.

Dinosaurs were not the only animals that grew very large. The fossils show there once were giant kangaroos, giant deer, giant birds, giant dragonflies, giant bears and bison. There were even giant beavers (eight feet long)! Even many plants grew much larger in ancient times. Perhaps the people were bigger, too. No one knows for sure, but it seems possible.

DINOSAURS IN THE GARDEN OF EDEN

In the original Creation dinosaurs were certainly not vicious or troublesome. When God finished making the animals He said they were *all* "very good." What colors were they? How different are the skeletons of dinosaurs we find killed by the Flood and those of the first dinosaurs created by God? Unfortunately, no one knows what Man or dinosaurs (or any other animals) *really* looked like when God first created them long ago.

Originally, dinosaurs must have been harmless—designed to delight man and benefit the world, just like all the other animals. When first created, all dinosaurs ate only plants and fruits.

DINOSAURS IN THE WORLD AFTER THE FLOOD

After the Flood, dinosaurs and all other animals were made to be afraid of people (Genesis 9:2). Animals stayed away from people if they could. They were no longer as trusting and obedient. God probably did this to protect both the animals and the people in the world after the Flood. Dinosaurs and Man probably lived in their own, separate areas— just like people and large, wild animals do today.

The fossil bones, teeth and stomach contents of many dinosaurs killed during the Flood have been found. So far, it appears that most dinosaurs were still harmless plant-eaters at that time—many hundreds of years after the Fall. They were probably not much different in their ways than a giraffe or elephant.

WHAT ABOUT THE TYRANNOSAURS?

The sharp teeth and claws of some dinosaurs have made people think that they were mean, vicious animals. The *Tyrannosaurus rex* is often pictured as a horrible killer, attacking every dinosaur in sight. But this may not be true at all.

New research suggests that the *Tyrannosaurus* would not be able to move very quickly. Most other dinosaurs could probably have gotten away from him easily. Fossil evidence indicates the *Tyrannosaurus* walked in a stooped-over (hunched) position and probably waddled like a duck.

There are other reasons to think that tyrannosaurs were not "super-killers." Their teeth were not rooted very well and might have snapped off in any real battle. *Tyrannosaurus rex's* small front legs seem far too weak for grabbing and killing large dinosaurs. In fact, they were too short to even reach his mouth.

If some of the dinosaurs we find killed by the Flood did eat meat, they were probably scavengers (like vultures) that lived off the bodies of large dead animals. So far, the fossil stomach contents of a tyrannosaur have never been found.

If we look at three other dinosaurs very much like *Tyrannosaurus*, even more problems can be seen with the idea that they were "super-killers."

1. Killing dinosaurs, biting through bones and tearing off hunks of meat should leave definite signs of tooth wear. Sometimes a tooth would even be broken or lost. An *Albertosaurus* (al-BERT-oh-SOR-us) was found with teeth that show almost no wear. The tips and the delicate edge serrations are said to be in almost perfect condition. Yet this tyrannosaur was an adult."

Did this dinosaur use its sharp claws for killing brachiosaurs? Or were the claws actually used for holding and eating certain types of plants and fruits? No one knows for sure.

2. The *Dilophosaurus* (die-LOAF-oh-SOR-us) had two high, paper-thin bone crests on its head! It doesn't seem very likely that this delicate head gear could keep from breaking off if the dinosaur made its living as a scavenger—greedily tearing into the insides of dead dinosaurs. If he was a fierce eater of *live* dinosaurs, the thin crests would certainly have been ruined.

3. The *Spinosaurus* (SPINE-oh-SOR-us) had long, delicate spines attached to its back bone. Some of these stood straight up in the air six-and-a-half feet high—taller than most men. These spines would have been very easy to damage in a fierce fight with a heavy dinosaur.

True fierce meat-eaters are smooth and sleek, like the tiger, lion, polar bear and wolf. They don't have any delicate spines or crests

to get in their way and cause them pain in a chase and fight. Perhaps the guess that tyrannosaurs were aggressive "brontosaur" killers is completely wrong.

Could it be that tyrannosaurs were mostly plant-eaters, not meat-eaters? The shape of their teeth alone can't tell us what they ate. Perhaps they used their sharp teeth and claws to tear up tough plants and fruits, not dinosaurs. Obviously sharp teeth can serve other purposes than simply cutting meat, just as kitchen knives can be used for cutting carrots as well as steaks.

Many sharp-toothed animals living today are plant-eaters and rarely (or never) eat flesh. A few of many examples include the Giant Panda, the large Australian fruit bat, and some apes and bears.

WHAT ABOUT TRICERATOPS?

Some dinosaurs, like the *Triceratops*, had bony spikes on their heads. Others had spikes on their backs and elsewhere. If basic types of horns and spikes like these were originally created by God, then we know something about their purpose. They were *not* meant for fighting other dinosaurs.

The head horns may have been used for getting food by lifting thick foliage. They could be used for poking, rooting or turning plants. Dinosaurs like the *Triceratops* had very strong jaws and replaceable teeth. Using their extremely strong jaw muscles, they could slice through very tough plants—even good-sized branches and roots. Dinosaurs like this could even have chewed on tree trunks.

Some insects have horns similar to those of dinosaurs. It is interesting that scientists used to think the big, sharp horns of some great horned beetles were meant for stabbing other beetles. Actually, the horns are mostly used to pry or lift.

DID ANY DINOSAURS EVER *BECOME* TERRIBLE AND FEROCIOUS?

The answer to this question remains a mystery. At this point, there is no proof that any of the dinosaurs were as mean and dangerous as shown in picture books. It will take many more discoveries before anyone can say for certain how dinosaurs behaved in the world before the Flood or after. However, it is likely that more people killed dinosaurs than dinosaurs killed people.

Bible-believing Christians can be sure of one thing. When dinosaurs were originally created, they were peaceful and harmless just like all the other animals.

DINOSAURS AND YOU: IMPORTANT THINGS TO REMEMBER

The Bible. Dinosaurs fit in perfectly with the Bible's record of history. Dinosaur-like animals are even mentioned in the Bible.

Creation. These wonderful creatures did *not* evolve from reptiles or amphibians. God created them perfectly finished. Today we can only guess what dinosaurs were really like in that sinless paradise of long ago.

The Creator. God's Son, Jesus Christ, created the great dinosaurs, the stars, and you (John 1:1-3). Since He made us, He owns us. He has the right to tell us what to do and how to live. God is the wisest and most loving being in the universe.

The Fall. Although everything God created was perfect, Adam and Eve chose to disobey God. Their choice brought death as a punishment for sin (Rom. 5:12).

Disobedience. All people have disobeyed God. Everyone has sinned, young and old (Rom. 3:23).

Sin Always Brings Pain. Adam's body was more perfect than ours today. He lived for 930 years before he died (Genesis 5:5). During his long life, Adam saw many sad changes in the living things under his control. Nothing was as perfect and wonderful as when God had created things (animals, plants, people or dinosaurs). In the years after Adam's death, things continued to grow worse. By the time of Noah, the whole earth was full of terrible sins and problems.

The Flood. Dinosaur fossils are reminders of the Great Flood when huge numbers of dinosaurs and millions of other animals were buried throughout the world.

God Punishes Sin. The Flood reminds us of God's punishment for sin—death.

God's Love. Jesus loves us more than we can understand. The Creator came down

to this world He made and became a human being. He became the first person to ever live a perfect life without sin. Jesus did this so that He could die for Adam's sins and yours. He took the punishment for our sins—the penalty we deserve.

Forgiveness and Eternal life. His amazing sacrifice can cover up each wrong we have done, so that God will forget them forever—even our worst sins. Then when we die, Jesus will welcome us to live forever with Him.

Creation Will Be Perfect Again. Jesus has something wonderful planned for those who are truly sorry for their sins and thankfully accept His gift of eternal life. God has promised to one day restore the Earth to the perfect, beautiful place it once was. The world will be the way God meant it to be. There will be no death, suffering or evil. It will be a world full of love, beauty, peace and fun. God will be in charge.

The animals will be as harmless and perfect as when they were first made (Isaiah 11:6-9). We will see the dinosaurs (and all extinct animals) in the way that God intended, not as dead bones, but as beautiful, living creations designed for our enjoyment. And Man will once again be able to rule with love and wisdom over all the animals, even the dinosaurs.

The Decision Is Yours. Don't be like the people at the time of the Flood that died in their sins. You can escape the punishment you deserve. By turning to Jesus, you can be forgiven and one day live forever in Paradise. There is nothing that you can do to save yourself. Only Jesus can save you.

Just believe Jesus and ask Him to forgive your sins. Thank Him for His love and ask Jesus to come into your life forever.

If you haven't done this yet, why not do it today? There is no better decision anyone can make.

INDEX